CW01395765

Published in the United Kingdom by;

themoneywonderland.com
Hastings
East Sussex UK

www.themoneywonderland.com

A CIP record of this book is available at the British Library

First printed February 2018

ISBN 978-1-9998485-0-7

Illustrations by courtesy of www.alice-in-wonderland.net

Printed in England by Berforts Ltd

Contents

Illiteracy, that curse of old,
Kept the people poor and cold,
Now ignorance of cash is used,
To keep the silly geese confused.

The Mad Hatter's Tea Party

"Money doesn't grow on trees," said Alice.
"Of course it does," retorted the March Hare scornfully.
"Money is paper and paper is made from trees. Everybody knows
that."

"Then how does it come to us?" asked Alice.

"You stupid child!" snapped the Mad Hatter. "The Bank
of Wonderland presides over money creation. First it declares the
value, and then it is lent out at interest."

"Why does The Bank declare that?" asked Alice.

"You must be very dull to ask that!" replied the March Hare.
"All kingdoms must do this. How else do you think the
population can buy and sell things?"

The Dormouse briefly woke at this point and
immediately fell asleep again.

"So if it is borrowed at interest, who pays it back ?"
asked Alice.

"Why the Population," retorted the March Hare, with an exasperated sigh. "You seem to have a very poor understanding of the simplest things."

"Well, who gets the interest when it's paid back?" asked Alice stubbornly.

"The men who create and lend the money of course," snapped the March Hare. "How else do you think they are able to buy their yachts and castles and all the kingdom's treasure?"

"Who are these people ?" asked Alice.

"Ask The Bank of Wonderland," retorted the Mad Hatter. "Although," he added darkly, "its workings are hidden by Royal Charter, and the Official Secrets Act, so you might not find much out."

"That can't be right," said Alice disapprovingly, "for if their activities were wholesome and proper, it would not be necessary to keep them secret."

"You must understand," continued the Mad Hatter, "the Bank of Wonderland is independent from any government control, and exists to look after the interests of the money people and their system."

"I think that's very unfair!" exclaimed Alice. "It costs hardly anything for them to print the money, yet when it's paid back, much value has been attached!"

At this the Dormouse gave a start and briefly woke up, but then promptly went to sleep again.

"That's right, go to sleep again, Pop," said the Mad Hatter. "He is very tired: he has to do all the work to make the money to repay all the debts."

"Why do you call him 'Pop'?" asked Alice.

"It's his name," said the Mad Hatter contemptuously. "It's short for Population."

"Well I think it's extremely unfair," said Alice in a determined way. "I can see no reason why the Population has to borrow worthless paper and pay it back with interest, after real value has been attached, that it didn't have in the first place."

"Also" asserted Alice, "I don't see why the Queen's Treasury can't print it. Why must the Population work hard only to yield up the national treasure to private and secret sources?"

"I would be very careful to whom you say that," said the Mad Hatter sternly. "A number of people have tried that in other countries, and curiously, it always seems to bring them very bad luck. I'm thinking of Mr Lincoln, Mr Kennedy and a number of other American presidents, and that's just one country. Then he went on to mention a number of unfortunate people from other places."

"Some of the people you speak of were not very pleasant," remarked Alice.

"Perhaps so, perhaps not," said the Mad Hatter curtly."But reputations must be destroyed and leaders dealt with if they threaten to enlighten the Population to the money trick."

"Remember," he continued "every newspaper and channel of information must be controlled tightly, and all key people bribed or blackmailed if word is not to get out."

"That's outrageous!"cried Alice loudly and decidedly. "Why they are nothing but knaves and tricksters and parasites. Dormouse for heaven's sake WAKE UP and send them packing!"

Oh tell me the truth about cash!

Is it only just simply a token,
To buy things we need to, and stash?
How on earth would we get on without it?
Please tell me the truth about cash.

Could buttons be used for this purpose
Or tally sticks fashioned from ash
If we say the object has value ?
Oh! please tell me the truth about cash!

Who is it that chooses its value?
Does the Queen dream it up in a flash?
Is it pulled from a hat like a rabbit?
Please tell me the truth about cash.

Does it spring from the air like a phantom,
When our fingers computer keys bash?
Do they know when enough has been printed?
Oh! Tell me the truth about cash!

And the money to pay for our projects,
All over the country to splash.
Must we borrow these tokens from bankers?
Oh! Please tell me the truth about cash!

When these tokens are seized by our taxes,
Causing everyone's teeth much to gnash,
Why use them to feather-bed bankers?
Oh! Tell me the truth about cash!

Is the Central Bank subject to no one,
Would to question it prove very rash?
Why is Parliament deaf on this subject?
Oh! Tell me the truth about cash!

If the banks produce money from nowhere,
How much would their profits be dashed
Should the nation take over this function?
Oh! Tell me the truth about cash!

What on earth would we do with the money,
Not to mention the interest we'd slash?
Would our days then forever be sunny?
Oh! Please tell me the truth about cash.

If, like Lincoln, we cut out the the bankers,
Would it certainly lead to a clash?
And for this have so many been silenced...?
Oh! Do tell me the truth about cash!

Who Stole The Tarts?

"Prisoner at the bar how do you plead? " demanded the King.

"I didn't steal the tarts. I purchased them" said the Knave, who was standing before the court in chains.

"You must plead 'guilty' or 'not guilty'," said the Queen petulantly. "We are not interested in your excuses."

"Well, if you did purchase the tarts," said the King suspiciously, "from whence did you get the money?"

"I didn't use money to buy them," said the Knave nervously. "I bought them with debt."

"That's a very stupid thing to say," said the King "and it proves you are guilty, for you cannot purchase things with debt: you have to use money. After all, and to be clear, and for the record, money is money and debt is debt."

"From whence did you get the debt?" demanded the Queen sharply.

"From the White Rabbit," said the Knave. "I bought his croquet set, but I didn't have any money, so I was left with debt."

"You can't buy things with debt," thundered the King in exasperation. "I say again, you must have money to buy things."

"Well, I turned the debt into money," whispered the Knave nervously.

"What a preposterous claim!" retorted the King. "Your defence is ludicrous, and very weak, and clearly you must be guilty. How on earth can you turn debt into money?"

"Oh, very easily" piped the Knave. "In fact it is happening all the time. Indeed there is no other way with our present system."

"You are on very shaky ground with that argument," retorted the King. "You are clearly clutching at straws."

"Unless you can explain yourself better to the Jury, we will get on with the sentencing," said the Queen impatiently.

"Well, I'll try " said the Knave hesitantly. "It is like this: whenever a person wishes to purchase an object, but hasn't enough resources, he must needs go to a bank and ask for a loan."

"Yes, yes! Get on with it!" cried the King impatiently. "Everyone knows that."

"Well," said the Knave very cautiously, "What actually happens next is the bank then pretends to loan the person some money, but astonishingly, doesn't lend anything at all. What in fact happens is that the person who goes to the bank to borrow, amazingly, gives the bank money instead. This he does over a period of time, as he can afford it, and always the amount he gives will exceed the original sum he asked to borrow: indeed, sometimes the amount he gives can total two or three times the amount he originally asked to borrow."

"Preposterous nonsense!" said the King.

"It's true! It's true !" pleaded the Knave excitedly. "The money doesn't really ever exist as money: it is really debt and it disappears when the person repays to the bank the money that the bank did not lend."

"I corroborate the testimony of the Defendant," declared the Mad Hatter.

"Strike those remarks from the record," said the Queen sternly. "The testimony of the last witness is not admissible. The Hatter is clearly mad."

"Oh dear! " said the King exhaustedly, "I must go and lie down in a darkened room, My head is spinning from trying to follow your argument. Usher, have you any aspirin?"

"I do sympathize" said the Knave consolingly. "You are not alone. The entire world is fooled by this conjuring stunt. You must understand that the process of turning debt into money was not designed to be logical, but designed rather to confuse and deceive. After all when you see a lady cut in half by a magician, you know it is a trick: you don't have to understand how the trick works to know it is a trick.

"Similarly, the bank, pretending to lend money it doesn't have, while receiving payment, and interest, for money it didn't lend, performs just such a trick. However, most do not even know that this is a trick, and of course very few understand how it works: and some who do," he added vaguely, "might say it is fraud."

"This is all very confusing," said the King. "We must have a qualified personage to give expert opinion on these matters. Call the Governor of the Bank of Wonderland."

There then entered a curious and mysterious figure.

"Are you the Governor of the Bank of Wonderland?" asked the King.

"I am, your Majesty," answered the new witness.

"Do you swear to tell the truth, the whole truth, and nothing but the truth, so help you God?" said the King.

"Do I really have to?" said the Governor.

"The penalties for lying are very severe," warned the King.

"But, my Lord my associates in the secret societies, to which I belong, and the secret services, might feel betrayed by me."

"I must warn you that the penalty for perjury in this court is death," said the King severely. "Answer me this: is all the money in our present system borrowed into existence?"

"This I cannot deny," agreed the Governor.

"And so it follows logically, that if everyone paid all the debts owed everywhere, all money would disappear, every penny?"

"Your Worship is correct in that assumption," confessed the Governor.

"This is a most remarkable state of affairs," said the King. "For what reason has the money system been designed in this way?"

"I would rather not answer that question, your Majesty," answered the Governor.

"The court insists you answer fully and with detail and upon pain of death," announced the Queen in a forthright manner.

"Very well," began the Governor slowly. "Were the money simply to be issued by the Treasury, without it first being borrowed, it would of course perform the same function, that is it would act as a token, to allow people to buy and sell things. However, things would then be very different. To begin with, those in high places, who organize the present procedure, would have no income and would have to go out to work. In addition, it would mean that your subjects might only have to work one or two days a week in order to keep themselves.

"At the moment most of the rewards your subjects get from their endeavours are collected in taxes, which are used largely by the Treasury to repay and service fictitious loans."

At this point Alice decided the whole extraordinary business was very disturbing. So she went for a walk to help her brain adjust to such an alarming concept.

The Gryphon Explains

As Alice left the court she fell into conversation with a Gryphon. "What I struggle to understand," she volunteered, "is how a third party or trader receives payment if the bank doesn't actually lend any money and the bank cheques are just thin air?"

"Firstly," replied the Gryphon, "you must understand; newly minted or printed money is worthless until its first use. At that precise moment it magically acquires the value of its first payment or trade.

"So, to answer your question: bank money, conjured out of virtually nothing, is used but it only achieves value after its initial use.

"Secondly, it is only after its initial use that it is logical and appropriate to charge interest for lending this money. This is the key to understanding the fundamental fraud systemic in banking.

"It would be appropriate for a bank to charge an administrative fee for its services, but never interest on non-existent money it hasn't lent.

"Oh! They claim they can loan out savers' deposits, and just keep back one tenth, because only one in ten savers will ever withdraw funds at the same time. They call this deception 'fractional reserve banking'. This is impossible because bank accounts are in continuous use. It is pure humbug and smoke and mirrors, to hide the plain fact they have taken over the government function of issuing brand new money tokens for which they, fraudulently, charge interest.

"The defence of the realm, and the establishment and maintenance of the currency are the two prime responsibilities of government. To hand control of either to private hands is high treason."

"Thank you for your revealing explanation," said Alice, as the enormity of this extraordinary fraud began to sink in.

14

Money Supply

If you wonder how our cash appears
The answer is - it hath two gears.

Gear One

The nation borrows ten percent.
Much from Central Bank is lent,
It writes out cheques for an amount -
But nothing's in its cheque account.

Yet our taxes will repay the loan,
With interest; so you never moan,
They call this process, 'selling bonds',
Such is the cloak this nonsense dons.

Gear Two

When rulers have this cash to spend,
'Twill into high street banks descend,
Where ninety more per cent will be
Conjured up with usury.

The Carnival of the Animals

They were indeed an odd looking party that assembled on the water's edge, the birds with dragged feathers, the animals with their fur clinging close to them.

"Can you recite to us something that is appropriate for animals while we dry?" said the Dodo. "Here, this will do," he said and handed Alice a manuscript entitled 'The Carnival of the Animals'.

Then Alice began to read it to them aloud.

A deer and a starling and a fish from a shoal,
All met in the pub to discuss protocol:
"To move in tight cluster and all turn as one,
Is essential for safety," they all said, "and fun."

A dog overhearing them held up his paw,
"What I enjoy most is defending my door;
I mark every lamp-post, establish a site,
Bravely awaiting each challenge to fight".

"What prompts you to do this?" asked a curious cat.
"It's simply an urge," they all answered back.
"We don't choose or think," they said at this junction,
"Like eating and drinking, 'tis a bodily function."

"Hmm" said the cat....

"To follow blind instinct is not always wise,
And refusing to think- that I really despise!
You are all very silly to limit your choice,
And sillier not to give reason a voice.

"In the 'eagle- and -wolf' days your stuff was OK,
But for 'net -and -the -gun' you are now easy prey.
And, as for you Fido, have you no wits?,
You never stop barking; you're simply a twit.

"There is only one creature more stupid than you,
It walks on two legs and it hasn't a clue,
With the mind of a parrot, for all it can say,
Are repeats of the soundbites the media play.

"A crafty old tapeworm directs all their action
Dividing them constantly into two factions:
Ensuring they always have someone to fight-
Their ultimate enemy hidden from sight.

"Terror for humans, albeit absurd,
Is to think for themselves, and step out of the herd;
They would much rather march, to be slaughtered as one,
Bomb mothers and children, use missile and gun.

"The Tapeworm has also come up with a wheeze,
To skim all the money, for him it's a breeze;
He's conned them to borrow, from him paper chaff,
With fictitious value, to buy and sell stuff!

"Did I mention before 'tis the tapeworm's own show?
He pulls all the strings, but prefers you don't know;
World leaders, and press, are tight in his grip,
'Tis verboten to carelessly let a word slip.

" 'Bye- bye', career is the price one must pay,
Should the truth ever meet with the cold light of day:
The Wizard of Oz tried to flag up this fiddle.
God forbid folk connect with the filmmaker's riddle.

"Before it's all borrowed 'tis just ink and paper.
But paid back with interest it rounds off his caper;
Then he uses their money to buy up their things-
And (don't laugh) 'tis simply a breathtaking sting.

"They must always pay back more than they get,
So can never, not ever, escape from the debt.
Print their own stuff and fix it? Show tapeworm the door?
No! These prize-winning twerps have their heads filled with straw.

"They think they're so clever, but live in a dream,
The poor things all suffer from 'high self-esteem';
Like peacocks they strut, all puffed up with pride,
Professors and experts - a huge rolling tide.

"Politicos too - the very best brains,
The Chancellor, PM and John Maynard Keynes:
It's hard not to laugh, for a cat not to smile,
For neglect of the obvious - they should be on trial!

"To give tapeworm his fix, folk must work off their pants,
Reducing mankind to the status of ants."

The Mock Turtle

They had not gone far before they saw the Mock Turtle, in the distance, sitting sad and lonely on a little ledge of rock, and, as they came nearer, Alice could hear him sighing, as if his heart would break. She pitied him deeply. "What is his sorrow?" she asked.

"He contemplates money," answered the Gryphon.

So they went up to the Mock Turtle, who looked at them with large eyes, full of tears, but said nothing.

"Could you describe money to us in simple terms?" inquired Alice.

The Mock Turtle sighed deeply, and drew the back of one flipper across his eyes. He looked at Alice and tried to speak, but, for a minute or two, sobs choked his voice.

At last the Mock Turtle recovered his voice, and with tears running down his cheeks, he began.

"Well, I'll try," said he. "To begin with, let us suppose that all things of value, in the Kingdom, were added up, and their monetary value totalled one million pounds."

"Yes, I'm with you so far," said Alice cautiously.

"Then," said the Mock Turtle, "tokens given the face value of one million pounds would have to be made available to permit things to get swapped around in the usual way of business."

"Of course," said Alice politely, although she thought that this was all very obvious.

"Well," said the Mock Turtle, "here the road forks, and this is the crucial heart of the matter, so please pay close attention."

"The old-fashioned choice was always to take the Right Fork: on this path, the Queen's Treasury created and issued the money, and spent it into circulation, both interest-free, and debt-free, for the public good.

"This resulted in everything always going on perfectly and forever. And there was never any inflation, which is a tax on everybody, and, of course, creates poverty.

"However," he continued, "things changed, for reasons that we won't address here, and the Left Fork was then chosen. This means that the currency is now borrowed, and at interest, from banks.

"And this is the crucial difference.

"This money now, of course, has to be repaid with interest.

"There is no point in logic or reason why this should occur, except to make some secret people rich.

"The results of this change are :

"One million pounds borrowed at, say, 10% per year would mean:

First, the whole of the million pounds would be gobbled up just paying the interest in 10 years;

Secondly, after 10 years, there would then be no money left for buying and selling things;

And, finally, the million pounds would still be owed."

"So, how is this remedied?" asked Alice.

"Well, the only solution with this system is called "The Bailout," continued the Mock Turtle.

"And this means more money must be borrowed to keep things afloat. This just means in reality that the debt, and debt repayments, are increased.

"Then when this extra infusion is used up in repayments, and the inevitable next insolvency crisis arrives, the solution is called 'Restructuring' the debt."

"This reasoning is getting very protracted," said Alice. "What does Restructuring mean?"

"It means reducing the rate of interest and providing a longer time to pay," said the Mock Turtle, "but in fact it results in enlarging the amount eventually to be repaid."

"I can't see that any of these measures would solve anything in the long term," said Alice.

"Finally," sobbed the Mock Turtle, "when the burden is so huge that repayments become totally impossible, the infrastructure of the kingdom - the roads, the airports, the docks, the railways - must all be yielded up in payment, and become the possessions of the lender."

"Oh, now I'm beginning to understand why you are so upset," said Alice.

"Why on earth is this not common knowledge," she cried, "and taught to every child from the age of five, and thundered from the newspapers? Where in heaven's name is the appropriate outrage? Is everyone asleep?"

Advice From A Caterpillar

The Caterpillar and Alice looked at each other for some time in silence. At last the Caterpillar took the hookah from his mouth, and addressed her in a languid, sleepy voice.

"What is it about the issue of money that you still don't quite understand?" he asked.

"Well, Sir, my confusion is this," Alice replied hesitantly.

"Should money be lent, then the lender has not the use of it, but transfers this benefit to the borrower; also there is a risk the debt may never be repaid. Therefore," she said "it seems to me entirely reasonable to make a charge for this arrangement."

"Ah", said the Caterpillar, "your confusion provides the veil behind which the money knavery hides and thrives."

"There is Money, and there is Debt which masquerades as Money," he continued, "and the two must never be confused.

"This confusion allows the wool to be pulled over everyone's eyes and the worldwide chicanery to thrive. What you expound are the principles upon which Building Societies once usefully, and honourably, conducted business.

"The logic you express is entirely appropriate for Real Money, that is moneys that have perhaps been spent into circulation, sans debt and interest, or earned, or perhaps are the proceeds of a sale," said the Caterpillar.

"But to confuse 'Bank money', which is Debt Money, with 'Real Money' is to confuse chalk with cheese, oil with water, heaven with hell, and is to be entirely humbugged. Bank money is fake money. It is Debt pretending to be Money, so it is negative money, or minus money, or created-from-out-of nothing money, or more accurately, created-out-of-less-than nothing money.

"It is just simply fraudulent to receive an interest payment for money you have not lent, but have tricked a victim into believing that you have."

"How much does interest matter?" asked Alice.

"As all money is borrowed into existence," answered the Caterpillar, "interest must be loaded into everything we buy, even a train ticket. It thus ensures money is transferred, automatically, from the very poor to the rich."

"Thank you, Sir,"said Alice, "for your good explanation, which makes it all very clear. However, there is one further matter which I find very muddling and upon which, perhaps, you might enlighten me."

"Allow me to consider your uncertainty" said the Caterpillar.

"Well", said Alice, "some insist money must always be exchangeable for precious metal, while others say money redeemable for nothing is the better choice. Can you tell me, please, which answer is correct?"

"There is but one straight answer to your question" replied the Caterpillar. "The supply of precious metal is not a constant; for instance, the production of gold can't keep pace with human expansion, and supply can also be erratic. Indeed, in the 1500s, gold increased in quantity, following the plundering of Central and South America, and this caused its value to diminish, it has been said, by 80%.

"So despite popular belief, 'Fiat Money' is the solution. This follows the principle made clear by Aristotle, who declared 'money exists by law and not by nature: it is not an item to be mined or farmed, but a token declared lawful tender by the state for trading, called 'Fiat money.'

"However, 'Fiat Money' must not to be confused with 'Fiat Debt Money.' Both have been employed in the past. The former is of great benefit to society, while the latter is always the bearer of poverty, inflation and misery for the people, and the provider of riches for the few who run the fraud."

"Thank you, Sir," said Alice, and she mused that what had at first seemed very complicated and confusing, was really very, very simple. "The only question now," said Alice, "is how might this outrage be rectified?"

"The usury propaganda and humbug of the banks, is exposed by the logic and reason of Aristotle and Plato. These wisest of all men decreed money-rules for us to use over 2000 years ago . Thus the remedy couldn't be easier or more simple," answered the Caterpillar.

"The re-introduction of the

BRADBURY POUND (technical name- MO)

would fix things in a trice. But first the public must become financially literate and demand it, a very difficult task because there are so many tight measures in place to suppress their awakening. If they only knew, the public would surely slay the monster with its enslaving alchemy to turn ignorance into gold. This offers a concise account." Then he began to recite his poem.

The Alchemist:
turning ignorance into gold

The banks usurp the right of kings
To create our money, and so bring
To everyone the usurers' yoke,
Enslaving all 'til all are broke.

To issue tokens is their scam,
With debt for money, so we can
Exchange debt tokens for a good:
Let this be clearly understood!

And for a "good" these tokens swap,
Pay heed! and let the penny drop.
For not until this act is taken-
And to this detail, please awaken

Doth the token value gain,
Around this fact please get your brain.
Before it's used it hath no worth
But on its use, behold the birth

Of value in the currency,
'Til then the token worthless be.
So how on earth can banks present
An interest charge when nothing's lent?

Now if you're shocked this news to get
You really ain't heard nothing yet.
The principal it must be paid
And into traders' hands be laid.

At very most an admin fee
Would fitting for their service be,
To let you have the thing you bought
And the pledge they from you sought.

But understand it's just the start
Of this amazing banking lark,
'Cos more and greater debt is lent
In ways that are completely bent.

Each time a bank receives some dough,
It's used for an excuse to throw
More phantom debt; they have the gall:
The people for this nonsense fall.

When cheques are to a bank returned
And, as described, have value earned,
This cycle will repeat once more
Though there's nothing in their store.

Then eight and twenty times repeat,
As waves upon the shore do beat,
Ghost money from thin-air next comes,
Let's total up and do the sums.

When ten thousand to bank is paid,
One hundred thousand can be made
Of phantom cash to fool us all,
While scheming bankers have a ball.

Should any lawyer, for a fee,
Charge bankers with grand larceny,
"Guilty" would decide the court,
If justice be not sold and bought.

The Tax that Dare not Speak its Name

"You said inflation is an invisible thief," said Alice. "Can you explain how it works, please?" "Poems are best," said the Caterpillar, "and this covers the subject satisfactorily." And so he began to recite.

'Inflation' is a secret tool
Designed, humanity to fool,
'Taxation' is the real name
For this cunning and deceitful game.

Alas! all prices rise and soar,
To catch up we must all work more:
We're told to blame the greedy men,
Who've hiked the prices up again.

This is a lie, and not the case,
The cause lies in another place,
The culprit is 'supply of cash',
Excess of this, our earnings trash.

When cash supply's increased it seems
A purchase will need further means,
The value of the good remains,
But what you've got to buy with wanes

In value. Though you scrimp and save
And beaver till you reach the grave.
This secret scheme will keep you poor
As up in smoke your savings soar

In income tax and V.A.T.
But the biggest grab you cannot see:
You can make a case for one and two,
The third is simply theft from you.

Were with tax this theft applied
'twould be for MPs' suicide,
And so they use this cunning plot
To hoover from us all we've got.

The answer is already found,
Just Google up 'The Bradbury Pound'
This tried and tested measure will
Inflation end, and soundly kill.

"The Governor said governments can't be trusted to supply money," said Alice.

"That's rich, coming from them!" retorted the Caterpillar scornfully. " History shows governments have a vastly superior record for inflation control. It's high time to bring back the **Bradbury Pound** and **To turn The tables.**"

The Caterpillar then recited this rhyme;

Inflation Control:

Usury   V   Honest Money
(no contest)

When money supply with debt is delivered
And only reined in when debt is paid down,
It's a rubbish arrangement when all is considered,
Which causes our floundering earnings to drown.
For the borrowing bit is ever the greater
Than the debt paid off, always tardy and later.

But money supplied from Treasury sources,
And extracted and balanced when tax is applied,
Will keep us all happy and save our resources,
Money pegged to a value and compelled to abide.
The inflationary robber is thus parked at zero,
The Chancellor then a national hero.

The Walrus and the Carpenter

"The time has come" the Walrus said
"For us to sit and muse
On where the crocodile gets his gold,
And who controls the news?

"Whence come the funds for wasting war?
To whom is interest paid?
Who pulls the strings to purchase strife?
And where should blame be laid?

"And who has this incentive
To bring war and debt about?
For they must work in secret
Or cat from bag will out."

"Well, look here," said the Carpenter,
What else can folk expect?
They deserve no more than oysters
If their brains they won't connect.

"It says here in the manual
It's by their own consent and choice,
They are but steaks upon a table
If in 'un-think' they rejoice."

"Silent Weapons For Quiet Wars,"
Go Google up and read,
To learn how genocide is planned
with wrenching, grasping greed.

The Rules of War

"Do you agree to abide by the Rules of War?"
asked the Red Knight.

"Certainly," answered the White Knight.

"Excellent," retorted the Red Knight. "Now, having agreed upon that, we can begin the fight."

"What nonsense you speak," said Alice, "there are no rules in war. War is horrid and very unfair: that the strong overcome the weak, is the only, very unjust, rule."

"Well, I noted that you wisely used the term overcome," said the Red Knight, "and did not speak of a winner; this is quite correct, as the overcomer can often suffer as much devastation and poverty as the defeated."

"Yes, the true winner is seldom one of the combatants," enjoined the White Knight.

"You speak in riddles," said Alice. "Whatever can you mean?"

"Why"said both of the knights together, "the winner of every war is the provider of the WAR LOANS of course !!!!"

"It is they that win every time," continued the White Knight. "It matters not which side claims victory - those that lend the money, especially to both sides, can never lose. First the devastation and then the reconstruction must be paid for."

"It is only when you come to realize this," said the Red Knight, "that you can grasp the real and hidden motive for all the seemingly unending, pointless and wasteful wars."

"Great poverty is visited on all sides engaging in warfare," said the White knight, "as every treasure must be yielded up to pay for the fighting. But this treasure does not disappear, as most assume; it just simply changes hands."

"Indeed", he continued "if you want to discover the true cause for any war, 'follow the money;' it's the best way to solve crime - ask any policeman. "

"And now on to War Rule 1," said the Red Knight, "this states that the first blow must always be self-inflicted."

"I can't see any sense at all in that," said Alice.

"Oh ! But one must always follow this rule and then claim to be innocent party, blaming your opponent for a cowardly, surprise, unprovoked attack. This will guarantee fear, self-righteous resentment, and a thirst for revenge from your followers," explained The White Knight.

"All wars have to begin this way, as otherwise you would never have an excuse to get them started" said the Red Knight. "The correct term for this manoeuvre among we military men is 'The False Flag Event'."

"These events require an awful lot of intricate planning" said the White Knight, "so it can't be surprising that those secretly organizing them often slip up, and flaws in the theatrical performances are clearly visible."

"All this is very disturbing," said Alice " and indeed shocking, and I do hope you do not have any further ghastly revelations to add to this."

"Well, perhaps just one" said the Red Knight. "You might perhaps call it War Rule 2. It is a useful stratagem when the public begins to become sceptical and lose interest. The remedy we employ then is the creation of a new, totally repulsive, manufactured enemy."

"Yes," said the White Knight, "this strategic tactic is invariably successful. But first you need to invent a catchy name for the new enemy - perhaps, for example, 'Crisis' could be appropriate.

"Then embed this catchy name in the nation that you plan to invade: those with hatred for you will flock to its ranks. Make sure your 'cloak and dagger' people arm and fund it well, then 'hey, presto', you can bomb and trash, murder and maim, without end, 24/7 in perpetuity.

"And, as a brilliant spin off, 'Weapons of Mass Migration' spring into existence, to destabilize and confuse efforts to oppose us at home."

"Oh! those poor refugees!" cried Alice, "Why this explains how, astonishingly, innocent people who would never dream of hurting anyone, risk everything, and are tricked into the wickedness and madness of war."

Seeing Is Believing

"Seeing is believing," said Alice.

" Rubbish," replied the Cheshire Cat.

"I see 'it' therefore 'it is,' " retorted Alice. And was very pleased and surprised to hear herself offer opinion in what she considered to be a grown-up and philosophical manner.

"What you see in your dreams you know to be fantasy upon waking," retorted the Cheshire Cat.

"We are fooled with illusion whilst sleeping," countered Alice, " but it can hardly be the case once one has risen."

"Most considering themselves awake sleepwalk," replied the Cheshire Cat scornfully.

"How can you justify such an extraordinary and sweeping statement?" asked Alice.

"The TV and radio and other measures are instruments used to induce myopia in the public," said the Cheshire Cat. "Every minute not working or sleeping, is spent gazing at a flickering glass image, which replaces talking, reading and thinking: it isolates the public from reality. In dreamlike semi-consciousness those watching all faithfully and naively accept, without question, everything they see. Mixed with genuine fact and twisted reality, and a huge amount of spurious rubbish, disinformation and downright lies are spoon-fed to the public."

"But who on earth would willfully orchestrate such a process," asked Alice, "and for what purpose?"

"Why, the deep state operating the fraudulent usury system, with its Orwellian goal of global enslavement," said the Cat. "They know if the public awakes, the game is over, so they make sure they control every source of information."

"How can this alarming process be avoided?" asked Alice.

"Throw your TV in the skip," replied the Cheshire Cat, "base your assumptions on evidence, and not on blind and lazy acceptance of media humbug; question everything, and examine the facts. Remember ignorance in the Information Age is a choice. I shall read my poem on this subject," continued the Cat, "inspired by Mr. Blake and his poem 'London.'"

He then began to recite his poem.

Manacles of the Mind

Inside a cage we keep our minds,
So we can be free,
From any thoughts that trouble us
Of sharp reality.

The wall we build to hide ourselves
From fresh ideas and thought,
Means efforts to enlighten us
Will always come to nought.

The easy choice to hide from truth
Makes fools of all mankind;
We dream and sleepwalk every day,
To key things we are blind.

With simple trust we take each word
Our leaders write and say,
Not dreaming it's a puppet show
Intended to betray.

All guided by a hidden hand,
Our welfare not to seek,
Just look at recent history
The havoc that is reeked.

We question not who rules the box
And tells it what to say,
The media target us with spin
To cloud our thoughts each day.

We crush each challenge to the truth,
Say "How can this be so,
The TV didn't mention it,
And surely they would know?"

Yet strangely we can clearly see
How folk are duped abroad,
And wonder how these silly clots
So brainlessly accord.

With lofty pride, we judge these "fools",
"How stupid they must be!
Told what to think by evil men,
With every word agree.

"Why can't these cretins see the light,
Be like us, see sense and reason?
We won't, of course, invade their land,
Well, not 'til the asset-stripping season."

Wake up! The tapeworm is in fear,
At just the very thought,
We waken to the money scam,
And justice might be wrought.

It's why the police now carry guns,
And the populous disarmed,
Why terror laws were introduced,
To frighten and alarm.

'Tis the pattern for us silly geese,
Through much of history,
The devil in the driving seat,
Minds made soggy with TV.

Latter-day Heresy

'What are those latter-day heresies you mentioned?"
asked Alice

"Impossible to divulge," answered The Red Queen.
"There are many and it is forbidden to speak of them."

"Well, perhaps could you just hint at one?" asked Alice.

"Usury is the key one," whispered The Red Queen, "break the
silence on this one and all the others, which are supportive of it,
will open like oysters."

"Usury, condemned in every religion, as sinful and evil, now is
never discussed. The subject appears strictly suppressed. Thus
there is no public awareness of the crime."

The Usurers' Prayer

Should any man or group feel free
To voice a modern heresy,
Please help us to get penetration
For control and damage limitation
Or, if single voice, elimination.

The group must then be steered away
So secrets can be made to stay
Hid from public scrutiny
Silenced must these voices be
And protest crushed effectively.

The "free-range tax farm's" conservation
Depends on human degradation.
And our 'fear and dumbing-down agendas'
In case the blighters wake and send us
Hence, from this O! evil one defend us.

The White Rabbit and the Train Set

"I would like to ask one more thing, " said Alice, as she spied the Caterpillar making for the royal kitchen garden.

"Could you explain please in simple terms, the process of conjuring money from nothing, in a way that can easily be understood by everyone?"

"Perhaps if I tell you a story," said the Caterpillar, "it will become clearer." He then began to tell the story, which he called:

The White Rabbit and The Train Set

And thus he began.

The White Rabbit looked through the window of the toy shop and saw a beautiful train set for sale, and its price was £90.

So he went to the bank, because he didn't have any money, to ask the bank manager if he could borrow £90.

The bank manager said, "I have only £100 deposited in the bank and it belongs to the March Hare. It's his salary, it comes in every month, and he spends it all on groceries, and train tickets, and the other things that he needs. So it's not possible to lend it out.

"However, I might be able to help you like this," he continued. "I could give you a piece of paper to say that the bank 'Promises to pay you £90', but you must give me a signed document, in return, to say that you will promise to pay the bank £90, plus interest."

This seemed to the White Rabbit a very good idea. So he signed an IOU, which is formally known as a promissory note. The White Rabbit and the bank manager then swapped these promissory notes, or IOUs, and although the bank had been asked for a loan, it didn't, actually, loan any money at all - what had occurred was just a swapping of IOUs.

At this point Alice looked startled.

"Ah ha!" said the Caterpillar, as he edged toward the cabbages, "I note your surprise. Wake up! Look at any bank note! Here is evidence of the money trick: although on this note it says, in large letters, "£5", the very small print says 'I promise to pay the bearer on demand the sum of five pounds'. So it isn't £5 at all but a promissory note to pay £5, or an IOU. The print is so tiny because the bank perhaps prefers that no one will ever read it. We misunderstand by calling it money when it is really only a promissory note."

Then he continued with the story.

The White Rabbit took the bank's promissory note to the toy shop manager who said, "That's good enough for me." So they swapped the bank's promissory note of £90 for the train set. (But understand that it was not until this instant that the bank's IOU acquired real value.) And the White Rabbit was very happy with the beautiful train set.

The next thing that happened was that the toy shop manager took the bank's promise to provide £90 and went to the bank. The bank manager said "The promissory note is clearly as good as money and works like money." So the toy shop manager deposited the bank's promissory note for £90 in the bank, and the bank manager agreed to pay 2% interest to the toy shop manager.

The White Rabbit, meanwhile, was as good as his word: he eventually paid to the bank the £90 that he had promised, as he could afford it, plus interest at 10%, and thus redeemed his IOU.

The consequences were:

(i) the toy shop owner got £90 and the White Rabbit a beautiful train set;

(ii) the bank conjured £90 in new money from thin air. It also gained the difference between 2% paid and 10% interest charged; and

(iii) the pool of money available for trading was increased by 90%. The value of goods remained stable, but the money pool was diluted, so buying power was diminished by the bank's inflationary process .

The Caterpillar then said to Alice:

"My grandfather told me that beer, in his youth, in the 1950s, sold at 8 pence a pint - but today a pint of beer is £4.50. Were the currency simply issued by the Treasury, beer would still be sold at eight pence."

Finally the Caterpillar said, "This tale is a story about usury. Remember usury is defined as charging excessive interest: therefore charging any interest at all for non-existent money, or just the promise of money, must certainly qualify as, and be, usury."

"Thank you for that lovely story," said Alice. "It is very revealing, but I'm still a little muddled."

"Do remember," said the Caterpillar, "the whole operation is designed to be confusing."

"Well, it seems to me ," said Alice, "that the bank's IOU cost nothing to produce, while the White Rabbit's IOU is backed by his future earnings: this hardly seems fair. I now understand how the bank just pretends to lend money, and bizarrely the borrower pays the bank money instead."

"It is as if by magic that the bank conjured £90 from nowhere, and this now belongs to the toy shop manager, while the bank gained a further £90 from the White Rabbit."

"Ah! the bank *receives* £90, it doesn't *gain* it," said the Caterpillar.

"Can you explain that to me please?" asked Alice.

"Please understand," said the Caterpillar, "the toy shop manager can withdraw his £90 at any time, so his deposit is a liability for the bank, while the White Rabbit's £90 payment becomes the bank's asset. Now this asset will balance the toy shop owner's deposit, so effectively the White Rabbit's payment becomes the money in the toy shop owner's account."

"Thank you," said Alice thoughtfully, "I think I've got it now; it's sinking in."

"Well, please also grasp," said the Caterpillar, "that this is just the first cycle of many to be repeated that will conjure, eventually, £1000 from the thin air, out of the original £100 deposited in the bank, as described in my alchemy poem."

"You began this book by asking if money grows on trees; well, for a very, very cunning few, it really does appear to. They seize all the earth's riches, with their money science. All governments have become their fawning servants, and humanity their slaves.

"A study of history will reveal that the true, but hidden, motive for nearly every war is the overthrow of each state that dares resist usury."

"That was never taught in my history lessons," said Alice indignantly. "What on earth can you mean?"

"Now, look here," replied the Caterpillar. "I'm very hungry and I want my dinner. There's pretty much everything in this book already for the readers to get a good grasp about how they are being mugged. You can fill in the detail in your next book of adventures. I'm famished." And with that he made his way off into the cabbages.

Are You Fed-up with Feeding the Fed?

"Can you skip?" asked the Frog."

Yes," replied Alice, "I like to skip."

"Here then take this," said the Frog, and he threw Alice a skipping rope. "We will keep together with this skipping rhyme," said the Frog.
"It's two skips and a jump per line."

So they began to skip together,
in perfect time, to these words:

Are you fed up with feeding the FED?
Does the tax it eats fill you with dread?
Should we print our own money,
Our days would be sunny,
But we borrow like donkeys instead.

Did you think that the old B O E
Was batting for just you and me?
Were you very much shaken
That you were mistaken
And it's playing for Team Usury?

Independent from Commons' control,
It dictates what the banks can out-roll,
Thus the banks can run free,
So, sod you and me,
Get us deeper in debt is their goal.

And to you it might come as a shock,
To find hidden under a rock,
Their anonymous clients,
In a secret alliance,
Concealing their deeds from the flock.

Does it come as a whopping surprise
To find all central banks are this wise,
And their sole occupation
Is to fleece every nation,
While the wolf wears a sheepskin disguise ?

Did you know that a spider resides
On a web over which it presides
Of the world's central banks,
Which fill up its tanks,
(An improvement on beetles and flies)!

Did you know that its location lies,
Not in some place in the skies,
But on the road to Lucern?
Where the BIS squirm,
Commanding the world in disguise.

When next time your MP you meet,
Ask politely of him as you greet,
That should he be frank
Re the old central bank
Would he get to hang onto his seat?

FED - Federal Reserve Bank
BOE - Bank of England
BIS - Bank of International Settlements

Summing Up

Usury, the secret tool,
Trashing nations one and all,
The 1% it can be said,
Keep people dumb, in fear and dread.

Illiteracy, that curse of old,
Kept the people poor and cold,
Now ignorance of cash is used
To keep the silly geese confused.

Illiteracy, that curse of yore
Kept the people starved and poor,
Now ignorance-with-cash remains
To keep the people bound in chains.

Illiteracy, in ages past,
In penury the people cast,
But understanding finance can
Free us from the money scam.

If we awake the fish to smell
And the guts to all and sundry tell,
Then those to come in future days,
Will live in peace and better ways.

Percentages

One percent the world controls,
Four percent have sold their souls,
Ninety slave in penury,
Five try to wake and set them free.
But the one per cent have hypnotised
The ninety to believe their lies.

The business of the usurer is the most hated, and with good
reason: for usury breeds money.
Money was designed for the purpose of exchange, and
not increase. The gain is not natural, as with breeding
plants or animals: the gain is at the expense of other men.

Aristotle Politics

Poem to Close

Gentle reader, if through these poor lines you happen to see,
Or just glimpse, the hidden reality;

And should you then wish to face and oppose
Those whom you knew not were your mortal foes;

And for sake of your loved ones and your kinder, stand
Against that grim future which for them is planned;

Then purchase five more of this brief, simple book
To send it to friends that they too might look.

Should there happen a birthday or Christmas come round,
Seize every occasion, the truth to expound.

Pray then that the scales shall fall from their eyes,
They awake from their sleep and the truth recognize,
And see behind the dread serpent's disguise.

It is nought but small effort and cash to expend,
The word so to spread and to bring to an end

The hopeless condition they've brought us all to,
Then the bars of our prison we can break our way through.

And the Devil shall know that we now have his number
And have wakened at last from our deep induced slumber.

John 2

14 *And found in the temple* ....*the*
changers of money sitting:
15 *And when he had made a scourge of small cords,*
he drove them all out of the temple,......................
and poured out the changers' money, and overthrew
the tables.

"By this means (fractional reserve banking), government may secretly and unobserved, confiscate the wealth of the people, and not one in a million will detect the theft."

John Maynard Keynes